CW00921171

Text: *Vivienne Crow*
Series editor: *Tony Bowerman*
Photographs: *Vivienne Crow, Carl Rogers, Stewart Smith Photography, Alamy, iStockphoto, Shutterstock*

Design: *Carl Rogers*

Northern Eye Books
ISBN 978-1-908632-01-2

A CIP catalogue record for this book is available from the British Library.

www.northerneyebooks.co.uk
www.top10walks.co.uk

Cover: *The Sun, Coniston (walk 1)*

This edition published in 2016 by
Northern Eye Books Limited
Northern Eye Books, Tattenhall, Cheshire CH3 9PX
Email: tony@northerneyebooks.com
For sales enquiries, please call 01928 723 744

www.northerneyebooks.co.uk
www.top10walks.co.uk

Twitter: @Viviennecrow2
@Northerneyeboo
@Top10walks

Contents

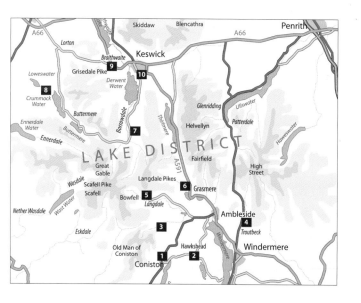

England's Largest National Park

THE LAKE DISTRICT NATIONAL PARK is the largest and most popular of the thirteen National Parks in England and Wales. Created as one of Britain's first National Parks in 1951, its role is to 'conserve and enhance' the natural beauty, wildlife and culture of this iconic English landscape, not just for residents and visitors today but for future generations, too.

Remarkably, the National Park contains every scrap of England's land over 3,000 feet, including its highest mountain, Scafell Pike. Packed within the Park's 885 square miles are numerous peaks and fells, over 400 lakes and tarns, around 50 dales, six National Nature Reserves, and more than 100 Sites of Special Scientific Interest—all publicly accessible on over 1,800 miles of footpaths and other rights of way. It's no surprise then, that the Lake District attracts an estimated 15 million visitors a year.

Little Langdale Tarn

Pub Walks in the Lake District

The words 'Lakeland' and 'pub' go together like 'bread' and 'butter' or 'Romeo' and 'Juliet'. It's a region of the country that's famed for its traditional inns and cosy, friendly village pubs almost as much as it's famed for its magnificent walking country. So, what could be better than combining the two—enjoying a pint of local ale half-way through a gorgeous Sunday stroll, or a hearty meal at the end of a day's hiking?

"The village inn, the dear old inn,
So ancient, clean and free from sin...
Ah, more than church or school or hall,
The village inn's the heart of all."

From *The Village Inn*, by John Betjeman, 1954

TOP 10 **Walks:** Pub Walks

THE TEN PUBS IN THIS BOOK have been selected partly on the basis of the fine walking that can be enjoyed from their doors and partly on the basis of their beer, their food and their warm Cumbrian welcomes. Open fires, exposed beams, beer gardens with mountain views, local produce, microbreweries, real ale... they're all here—as are low fells, hidden tarns, fertile valleys, sparkling lakes and picturesque villages. The perfect combination!

page 8
page 14

page 20

page 26

Old Dungeon Ghyll, Great Langdale

page 30

Tweedies Bar, Grasmere

page 36

Langstrath Country Inn, Borrowdale

THE LANGSTRATH COUNTRY INN

Food • Drink Accommodation

1/2 mile

page 42

Kirkstile Inn, Loweswater

LOWESWATER GOLD

BREWED IN THE LAKES
ABV 4.3 %

page 48

Middle Ruddings Inn, Braithwaite

page 52

Dog & Gun, Keswick

DOG & GUN

Free House & Dining

page 58

Coppermines Valley

The Sun
Coniston

What to expect:
Woodland, low fells and valley tracks; clear paths; rocky section on ascent

Distance/time: 9km / 5½ miles. Allow 3¼-3¾ hours

Start: Main pay and display car park near the Tourist Information Centre in Coniston

Grid ref: SD 303 975

Ordnance Survey Map: OL6 The English Lakes South-western area, *Coniston, Ulverston & Barrow-in-Furness* and OL7 The English Lakes South-eastern area, *Windermere, Kendal & Silverdale*

The Pub: The Sun, Coniston, Cumbria LA21 8HQ | 015394 41248 | www.thesunconiston.com | info@thesunconiston.com

Walk outline: The Yewdale Fells are low-lying, grass-topped hills just to the east of the higher Coniston mountains. The walk skirts the edge of this peaceful area, having approached via the Yewdale woods and then climbed through the now silent Tilberthwaite quarries. It finally descends into the Coppermines Valley, under the watchful gaze of the imperious Old Man.

On the edge of Coniston, The Sun is a traditional inn with a lovely, hospitable feel. With stone floors, warming fires and exposed beams, it's everything you'd expect of a village pub. Gaze across the fells while enjoying simple, tasty meals.

400 year-old Inn

► The Sun at a glance

Open: Daily, 12 noon-11pm

Brewery/company: Free house

Real ales: Black Sheep plus various beers from Coniston, Barngates, Skipton, Hawkshead and Keswick breweries

Food: Daily, 12-2.30pm, 5.30-8.30pm. Decent children's menu and selection of lighter meals. Large groups are advised to book

Rooms: Eight en-suite rooms

Outside: Sun terrace with 20 tables

Children & dogs: Children and dogs on leads welcome

The Walk

1. From the main car park in **Coniston**, turn left along the residential road and, almost immediately, left along the B5285, passing the **Crown Inn** on your right. At the T-junction, turn right and then left, immediately after the **Black Bull** pub.

Where the surfaced lane goes over to a rough track, turn right—signposted to 'Yewdale, Elterwater and Ambleside'. With craggy ground up to your left, the clear path skirts the base of the **Yewdale Fells** and then enters the woods, running parallel with the A593.

2. It eventually drops on to the minor road to **Tilberthwaite**, close to its junction with the **A593**. Turn left along the Tilberthwaite road and walk along the asphalt for about 650 metres.

3. Turn left at a fingerpost—along a wide, muddy track—signposted to 'Coniston and the Yewdale Fells'. Roughly 300 metres after joining this track, just as it swings left, take the narrow trail off to the right. As you climb towards the disused **Tilberthwaite quarries**, you will have to negotiate some rocky outcrops as well as two gills.

The eastern fells can be clearly seen as you gain height.

As you pass close to the edge of a large, open pit on your right, the path swings left and joins a clearer route coming up from the right. This now heads up the side of **Tilberthwaite Gill**, the ground on your right dropping away steeply into the dark, tree-shrouded ravine.

To the fells: *Heading on to the Yewdale Fells from the Tilberthwaite road*

4. As you near the top of the gill, the path swings left. As it does so, keep left at the fork—ignoring the right-hand branch, which drops to ford the beck.

With Wetherlam's steep, craggy slopes soaring up to the right, everything at this level inevitably seems diminutive—from the sheep to the lonesome walker moving through this imposing landscape.

Skirting the edge of the **Yewdale Fells**, the path at first maintains just enough height to avoid the boggy ground in the base of this hanging valley. Then, soon after fording a tributary beck, it climbs gently to a pass that is home to a shallow, reedy tarn.

Descending the other side of Hole Rake, the views open out in dramatic fashion with Morecambe Bay visible in the distance. *On the far side of Coppermines Valley is the eastern face of the Old Man, scarred by generations of mining and quarrying.*

There is evidence of copper mining in the Coniston area as far back as 1599. This

Wide panorama: *Looking south across Coniston and the Grizedale Forest*

was a few decades after German miners, regarded as the best in Europe, had been invited to England by Elizabeth I. Employed by the Company of Mines Royal, they established copper and lead mines throughout Cumbria.

The mines were at their most prosperous during the middle of the 19th century, when as many as 600 people worked in the Coppermines Valley. But growing imports of cheap ore from abroad in the 1880s marked the beginning of the end. The pumps were finally switched off in 1892

and, within five years, most of the mine had filled with water.

5. Dropping on to a track close to yet more disused quarry workings, turn right. Follow this round to the left in a short while. You are then joined by a track coming in from the right and together you drop on to a wider track in the valley bottom. Turn left along this and, in 150 metres, go through the gate on your right to cross **Miners Bridge**. On the other side, turn sharp left to follow **Church Beck** downstream along a broad, stony track along the top of the gill.

6. The track ends at a group of farm buildings at the edge of **Coniston**. Bear right along the surfaced lane here. When you reach the road, **The Sun** is on your left. From the pub, turn left to drop to the main road through the village. Turn left at the T-junction—over the bridge—and immediately right to retrace your steps to the car park. ♦

Coniston and the Campbells

Donald Campbell broke four water-speed records on Coniston Water before his famously ill-fated attempt to break the 300 mph barrier in Bluebird K7 on January 4, 1967. But he wasn't the first Campbell to break records on the lake: his father, Sir Malcolm Campbell, achieved a record-breaking 141.74 mph on August 19, 1939 in Bluebird K4. Donald's remains were finally recovered in 2001, and he was later buried in the local cemetery.

Stone pillar on the summit of Latterbarrow

Queen's Head
Hawkshead

What to expect:
Field paths; quiet lanes; woodland; low-lying grassy fell

Distance/time: 7km / 4¼ miles. Allow 2¼-2¾ hours

Start: Main pay and display car park in Hawkshead

Grid ref: SD 353 980

Ordnance Survey Map: OL7 The English Lakes South-eastern area, *Windermere, Kendal & Silverdale*

The Pub: Queen's Head, Main Street, Hawkshead, Cumbria LA22 0NS | 01539 436271 | www.queensheadhawkshead.co.uk | info@queensheadhawkshead.co.uk

Walk outline: Latterbarrow makes for a popular walk from busy Hawkshead. And for good reason too: the views from this little bump in the landscape are totally out of keeping with its rather paltry 244 metres of height. From the village, it's a short walk across fields and along lanes to reach it. After a short, moderate climb, the return is via forest.

The warm and cosy Queen's Head in Hawkshead has been welcoming weary travellers since the early 17th century. Visitors can relax in the wood-panelled surroundings of the friendly bar or eat in the more formal dining area. The seasonal menus are largely sourced from local farms and estates.

Hand-painted inn sign

▶ Queen's Head at a glance

Open: Mon-Sat 11am-midnight; Sun 12 noon-11pm
Brewery/company: Robinsons
Real ales: Robinsons' Dizzy Blonde and Double Hop; Hartleys' Cumbria Way; guest beers
Food: Mon-Fri 12-2.30pm, 6.15-9.30pm; Sat 12-4.30pm, 6.15-9.30pm; Sun 12-5pm, 6.15-9.30pm. Booking recommended
Rooms: 13 en-suite rooms
Outside: Small area with tables
Children & dogs: Children welcome. Dogs allowed in bar only

The Walk

1. From the car park, follow signs into the village, soon walking between the **National Trust shop** and the **Queen's Head**. Just after the **Red Lion's beer garden**, turn right along a lane and, as this ends, swing left through a gate. Cross the road and take the track opposite. After the beck, turn left. Follow the path to a small gate and then continue in the same direction to another gate. Beyond this, bear left. Turn left along a rough track and then right, through a kissing-gate.

2. On reaching the road, turn right. At the T-junction, turn left and then right through a gate. When the clear path forks, bear left to climb more steeply to the tall stone column on top of **Latterbarrow**.

With no other high ground nearby, the views in all directions are far-reaching. They include the Coniston Fells, Crinkle Crags, the Langdale Pikes and the Fairfield Horseshoe.

3. From the top, swing half-right to follow a path downhill, heading south. Cross the stile and walk through the woods. Soon after a gap in a wall, go over a track crossing and follow the path as it winds its way over a small, felled hill. On reaching another wall, it swings right for a few metres and then crosses a gap in the wall—down some steps. Crossing an open area, it then climbs back up to the forest proper.

4. Turn right along the track. Take either option whenever it forks.

5. On reaching the road, turn left and then right along a narrow lane. Seventy metres beyond the junction, turn left at a fingerpost and through a gate.

Chalk and cheese: *Looking across the rolling farmland around Hawkshead*

Swing right to walk with a fence on your left and then go through a gap in the wall. There isn't an obvious path, but if you look to the west, you will see a yellow-topped marker post. Make your way over to this and then continue west, past the next marker post and across a stile in a wall. Follow the path downhill to **Scar House Lane**.

6. Go straight over the track and through a kissing-gate a little to the right. Bear left at the next junction of paths, and go through the kissing-gate to retrace your steps to the car park. ♦

Picturesque village

Said to be named after a Norseman called Haukr, pretty Hawkshead has existed since the 10th century. It is an attractive, jumbled muddle of narrow alleyways, low archways, timber-framed buildings and a market square. The market, originally an important centre for the wool trade, was first established by the wealthy monks of Furness Abbey. At one time, the monks owned all the land in this area.

Slaters Bridge, Little Langdale

Three Shires Inn
Little Langdale

What to expect:
Mostly stony tracks; a path along the base of the fells; quiet lanes

Distance/time: 10km / 6¼ miles. Allow 3½-4 hours

Start: Tilberthwaite car park, about 3.5km north of Coniston

Grid ref: NY 306 009

Ordnance Survey Maps: OL6 The English Lakes South-western area, *Coniston, Ulverston & Barrow-in-Furness* and OL7 The English Lakes South-eastern area, *Windermere, Kendal & Silverdale*

The Pub: Three Shires Inn, Little Langdale, Cumbria, LA22 9NZ. 015394 37215 | www.threeshiresinn.co.uk | enquiry@threeshiresinn.co.uk

Walk outline: This scenic walk takes in some varied terrain: from old quarry tracks to a secret path at the base of Lingmoor Fell and some delightful sections of woodland. The views are constantly changing as it makes its way from Tilberthwaite, near Coniston, down into sleepy Little Langdale and back via the impressive remains of the old Hodge Close quarries.

This small, slate-clad inn sits in a peaceful spot in scenic Little Langdale. A lively menu offering both traditional (beef and ale pie) and modern food (Thai sweet chilli noodles) can be washed down with a wide selection of beers, whiskies or wines.

Three Shires Inn

▶ **Three Shires Inn at a glance**

Open: Mon-Thurs, 11am-10.30pm; Fri & Sat, 11am-11pm; Sun 12 noon -10.30pm

Brewery/company: Free house

Real ales: Beers from Jennings, Hawkshead, Coniston, Ennerdale, Cumbrian Legendary Ales and Barngates

Food: Daily, 12-2pm, 6-9pm; booking recommended

Rooms: Ten en-suite rooms

Outside: Small beer garden with six tables

Children & dogs: Children welcome in bar until 9pm. Dogs welcome

The Walk

1. From the National Trust parking area in **Tilberthwaite**, turn left along the road. On reaching the end of the road at **High Tilberthwaite Farm**, enter the farmyard and head for the track going uphill through a gate beside a low building on the left. This wide, stony track climbs slowly.

2. Dropping into **Little Langdale**, turn left at a junction with another clear, stony track—signposted to 'Fell Foot'. Bear right at a fork.

3. Turn right when you reach the road and then, just before a cattle grid, take the road on the left—signposted to 'Blea Tarn and Great Langdale'. After about 180 metres, turn right along a grassy track, which has a low wooden barrier across it. You climb briefly and soon have a wall on your left. As the wall starts to climb away from the path, another comes up from the right. Just after a kissing-gate, ford a small beck. Don't be tempted by the rock chute heading straight up the slope here; instead, turn right immediately, clambering over some rocks to gain a narrow, beckside route. As the beck quickly swings away, you rejoin the line of the wall on your right.

This pleasant path, skirting the base of **Lingmoor Fell**, is mostly easy underfoot, but it does become a little rougher after passing the buildings at **High Bield**, where it briefly climbs more steeply. Keep to the path nearest the wall and you will eventually reach a gate. Ignore the path heading steeply up to the left here; instead, go through the

0   1km
1 mile

Into the valley: *Little Langdale and Wetherlam*

gate to continue in roughly the same direction. The clear path drops to a track.

4. Turn left here. In 250 metres, go through the gate on your right—signposted to 'Wilson Place'. Ignore the track to the left early on. After this, it is hard to go wrong as the clear path drops to the farm via a series of gates. Swing left through the farmyard and then turn right along the road to reach the **Three Shires Inn**.

Beyond the pub, turn left along a surfaced lane—towards Tilberthwaite and Coniston. Cross the **wooden footbridge** at the end of this lane.

5. Ignoring the track on the right, walk straight ahead, but then, immediately after the short stretch of wall on the left, turn left along a narrow trail through the trees. This runs alongside the beck at first, but then swings right. It comes out on to a surfaced lane, along which you turn left. The lane climbs and bends sharp right near the buildings at **Stang End**. Turn right along a rough track

Stunning view: *Little Langdale Tarn is ringed by high fells*

here—signposted to 'Hodge Close and Coniston'.

The track passes through several gates before it reaches the cottages at **Hodge Close**. Keep to the surfaced lane, which passes close to an enormous quarry pit.

Be very careful if you decide to explore this area—with little warning, you can find yourself on unstable ground at the top of a steep drop. This massive excavation has resulted in sheer sides that are popular with abseilers. Divers too find plenty of interest here: the blue-green quarry pool is more than 30 metres deep in places and there is an underwater entrance that leads to three chambers and two interconnecting tunnels.

6. As the lane swings right at the far end of the pit, leave it by striking off left. There is no path on the ground here at first, but you soon reach a gate. Go through it to access National Trust land at **Holme Fell** and turn right along the woodland track. This heads gently uphill for about 650 metres. When it starts descending, you will see a farmhouse on the road below. You pass above the farm and drop to a wall. Now turn sharp right, and follow the grassy track to the farm.

7. Turn left at the road. About 200 metres beyond the buildings, turn right at a fingerpost and through a gate into the woods. Just before the path drops to a gate, bear left at a waymarker.

A faint path heads up the wooded slope and then drops to a kissing-gate. Once through this, walk with the beck on your left and then turn left along the road to return to the parking area. ♦

The Quarries

Two World Wars hastened the end of quarrying at Hodge Close. With the men away from 1914 to 1918, the steep walls became unstable and rock falls damaged the equipment below. Eventually, the pumps were stopped and water slowly filled the pits. Quarrying restarted when the men returned in 1918, but then there was a repeat performance during the Second World War. Hodge Close Quarry was finally closed in the 1950s.

Ill Bell rising above the head of the Troutbeck valley

The Mortal Man
Troutbeck

What to expect:
*Good valley tracks;
farm path; quiet lanes*

Distance/time: 8.5km / 5½ miles. Allow 2½-3 hours

Start: Small parking area near Troutbeck village. If driving south along the A592, turn right 120 metres after passing the church on your right. The parking area is on the left beside Trout Beck

Grid ref: NY 412 027

Ordnance Survey Map: OL7 The English Lakes South-eastern area *Windermere, Kendal & Silverdale*

The Pub: The Mortal Man, Troutbeck, LA23 1PL | 015394 33193 | www.themortalman.co.uk | reservations@themortalman.co.uk

Walk outline: If you're searching for the Lake District idyll, you'll probably find it on this gentle exploration of the Troutbeck valley. The walk first heads up the eastern side of the valley, into wild country beneath steep-sided fells. It then returns to the beautiful, historic village of Troutbeck, surrounded by drystone walls that dissect the rolling farmland into tiny enclosures.

The Mortal Man sits part way up the hillside, overlooking gorgeous fell and dale scenery. An inn since 1689, it continues to pride itself on its warm hospitality, good range of beers and tasty food today.

Pub sign and rhyme

▶ The Mortal Man at a glance

Open: Daily, 12 noon -11pm
Brewery/company: Enterprise
Real ales: Loweswater Gold, Coniston Bluebird, Loughrigg (Hesket Newmarket Brewery), Sally Birkett's Ale, Timothy Taylor's
Food: Mon-Fri, 12-2.30pm, 5.30-9pm; Sat and Sun, 12-4pm, 5.30-9pm. Bar meals or more formal dining in the Garburn restaurant
Rooms: Twelve en-suite rooms
Outside: Large beer garden voted one of top 15 in the country
Children & dogs: Both welcome. No dogs in restaurant

The Walk

1. From the parking area, turn right along the lane and then left at the main road, quickly passing the pretty **Jesus Church**.

This stands apart from the village because it once served both Troutbeck and Applethwaite. It is thought there was a

chapel here as early as 1506, but the whole church was dismantled and rebuilt in 1736. Probably the most famous feature of the church is its east window, a large and colourful stained glass by the Victorian artist and designer Sir Edward Burne-Jones and made by William Morris & Co. Some of the detail is the work of pre-Raphaelite painter Ford Madox Brown. Local legend has it that designer William Morris and Ford Madox Brown came to Troutbeck on a fishing holiday while Burne-Jones was working on the window, and they stayed to assist him.

About 200 metres beyond the church, turn right into **Limefitt Park**. Follow the main driveway through the site, across **Trout Beck** and up to the right of the **Haybarn Inn**. Go up the steps and bear left around the back of the building—along a signposted bridleway.

2. Climb gently to a large wooden gate at a junction of paths. Turn left to go through the gate. You are now on a clear bridleway that you follow up the valley for 3.5 kilometres.

The mountains up to the right of the head of the valley belong to the western arm of the Kentmere Horseshoe: Yoke, Ill Bell and Froswick. Sitting at their feet is The Tongue, a mere sliver of a fell that is cradled by

0   1km
         1 mile

Centre stage: *Heading towards the top of the Troutbeck Valley with The Tongue ahead*

its much loftier, altogether more serious neighbours. Our route takes us right up to the base of The Tongue.

Almost 500 metres after passing **Long Green Head Farm** on your left, make sure you are not tempted by the track heading down through the gate to the left; you need to keep to the right of the wall. You will eventually see a wooded gorge to your left, beyond which you should ignore the path to the left

dropping down to a bridge over **Hagg Beck**. Continue upstream for a few more hundred metres, along a now grassy track that passes below some disused quarry workings and into the ever wilder valley.

3. Cross the next bridge close to an old stone barn and then climb to a gate. Once through this, turn left along the clear track—along the base of **The Tongue**—to begin the return route. After passing through a gate, ignore the path down to the left, but then go through the next kissing-gate on your

Grand valley: *The head of the Troutbeck valley is backed by the Kentmere Fells*

left—signposted to 'Troutbeck village'. Head straight down the grassy slope on an indistinct path (heading south-west) that passes to the left of a small rise. Looking to the right now, you can see **Troutbeck Park farm**.

4. When you reach a surfaced lane, turn left along it. This quickly crosses **Hagg Bridge**, followed later by **Ing Bridge**. Having passed a small stone building on your left, bear left along a track. Confined by walls and fences on either side, this climbs easily to the main road.

5. Go straight over and follow this lane round to the right in a short while— signposted for 'High Green'. Bear left at the next junction to reach **The Mortal Man** pub.

6. The route then bears left at the junction above the pub. This quiet road goes right through **Troutbeck**, passing several interesting cottages.

Among the many buildings with a story to tell is Hoggart's House, near Nanny Lane. This is named after playwright Thomas Hogarth, who lived here in the 17th century. 'Auld Hoggart', as he was known, was the uncle of the 18th-century

painter and cartoonist William Hogarth. He achieved some notoriety locally with his bawdy poems.

Follow the road for 900 metres and then take the next road on the left—just before the **Post Office**. This winds its way downhill and eventually drops back to the parking area where the walk started. ♦

Potty about Herdies

Beatrix Potter is, of course, best known as a writer and illustrator of children's books, but she was also president of the Herdwick Sheepbreeders' Association. Having bought the 1,900-acre hill farm Troutbeck Park in 1923, she ran the place with the help of shepherd, Tom Storey. The pair established a celebrated flock of Herdwick sheep, the hardy Cumbrian fell breed, and its success resulted in her appointment to the breeders' society.

Mickleden valley in high summer

Old Dungeon Ghyll Hotel
Great Langdale

What to expect:
*Valley paths and tracks;
often rough underfoot;
one significant ford*

Distance/time: 7km / 4¼ miles. Allow 2¼-2¾ hours

Start: National Trust pay and display car park at the Old Dungeon Ghyll Hotel, Great Langdale

Grid ref: NY 286 060

Ordnance Survey Map: OL 6 The English Lakes South-western area. *Coniston, Ulverston & Barrow-in-Furness*

The Pub: Old Dungeon Ghyll Hotel, Great Langdale, Ambleside, LA22 9JY | 015394 37272 | www.odg.co.uk | olddungeonghyll1@btconnect.com

Walk outline: Who says valley walks can't be just as inspiring as hikes on the open fells? This route never climbs above 140 metres and yet, towered over by soaring peaks, it is breathtakingly beautiful. It explores the head of Great Langdale and Mickleden. A wide beck has to be forded part-way through the walk, but this shouldn't present any difficulties except after heavy rain.

Beloved of many generations of fell-walkers and climbers, the iconic Old Dungeon Ghyll Hotel lies at the head of Great Langdale. Its popular Hikers' Bar may be basic and its food simple, but you really can't beat it for atmosphere.

The famous Hikers' Bar

▶ Old Dungeon Ghyll Hotel at a glance

Open: Mon-Sat, 11am-11pm; Sun, 11am-10.30pm

Brewery/company: Free house

Real ales: Black Sheep Bitter, Yates Bitter, Jennings Cumberland Ale and Theakstons Old Peculier. Also, three guest ales and a guest cider

Food: Daily 12-2pm, 6-9pm. Hearty, tasty pub grub in simple surroundings. No booking

Rooms: 13 bedrooms, including four en-suite

Outside: Beer garden with 17 tables

Children & dogs: Children welcome until 9pm; well behaved dogs at all times

Mountain valley: *Mickleden is dominated by Bowfell and Rossett Pike*

The Walk

1. From the National Trust's **Old Dungeon Ghyll car park**, follow the surfaced lane around the side of the Hikers' Bar and the back of the hotel. When it swings right, bear left along a rough track leading to a gate. Once through this, bear right on a rough path that swings right and climbs to another gate—hidden from view at first. Go through this to follow a rough path along the base of the fells and with a wall on your right. Soon after crossing a beck via a bridge, the path climbs to a kissing-gate. Just after this, go through the gate on your right and follow the muddy path steeply down into another National Trust car park—this one close to the **New Dungeon Ghyll Hotel**.

2. Leave the car park via its vehicle entrance and turn left along the road. In about 30 metres, turn right along a farm track—signposted 'Oak Howe'. Go through the gate to the left of the buildings at **Side House** and then cross the plank bridge. Bear right to follow a small beck upstream for about 50 metres and then cross the bridge and ladder stile over the wall on your right.

3. Contouring the hillside on a narrow but clear path, you cross a second ladder stile and then the remains of an old wall. Soon after this, bear left along a less obvious path heading slightly uphill. The route on the ground is unclear, but you should try to walk parallel with the fence that is up the hill to your left. Before long, you pick up the line of a fence on your right and go through a kissing-gate. Continue alongside the fence until you reach a wall.

4. Turn right through the gate and descend. After the next kissing-gate, swing half-right down the grassy slope to pass through a gap in a wall followed

by two gates in quick succession to enter the **National Trust campsite**. Go straight over at a crossing of paths and then turn left along a track, soon leaving the campsite via a gate.

5. Turn right along the road and, at a sharp right-hand bend, turn left along a surfaced farm track.

You are now looking straight up towards the head of Oxendale backed by the impressive buttresses of Crinkle Crags, home to some of the finest high-level walking in the entire Lake District. These are truly magnificent surroundings.

The track leads right up to **Stool End Farm** where you need to keep a close eye on the signposts guiding you

Impressive dale head: *Mickleden is ringed by some Lakeland's most famous fells: Crinkle Crags, Bowfell and the Langdale Pikes*

between the farm buildings. The right of way swings right and then left, climbing to a gate to leave the farmyard.

6. Beyond the gate, turn right to walk on with a wall on your right.

Ahead of you now is the valley of Mickleden with Rossett Pike and Rossett Gill at its head. On the other side of the valley, the impossibly steep, scree-ridden slopes lead up to Gimmer Crag and Pike O'Stickle.

Soon after a kissing-gate, the path swings slightly right to pass between two walls. When the wall on your right swings away, keep straight ahead for a few more metres, but then, when the main track swings left, bear right along a narrower path that soon runs parallel with the beck.

7. You now need to ford **Mickleden Beck**. Just upstream of the abutments of the old bridge is a weir. As long as you aren't attempting this walk after heavy rain, you can easily cross the top of this, but be careful because the submerged stones are slippery. Once across, make

straight towards the steep slopes ahead. In about 120 metres, you reach a track, along which you turn right. After one and a half kilometres, you will see the buildings of **Middle Fell Farm** to the right. Don't be tempted by the track down to the farm; continue with the wall on your right until you reach the gate behind the Old Dungeon Ghyll Hotel. Go through this and drop back on to the lane leading down to the car park where the walk started. ♦

Prehistoric axe factory

High up on Pike o' Stickle, Neolithic stone workers once quarried an exposed seam of 'greenstone'. It's a hard, flint-like volcanic rock that they made into beautiful polished axe heads. There was a significant trade in these status symbols and Langdale axes have been found as far away as Cornwall. The prehistoric 'axe factory' is on a steep and unstable scree and a visit is not recommended.

Helm Crag from the Alcock Tarn path

Tweedies Bar
Grasmere

What to expect:
Low fells and woodland; mostly clear tracks and paths; steep ascent

Distance/time: 8km / 5 miles. Allow 3-3½ hours

Start: St Oswald's parish church, Grasmere

Grid ref: NY 306 225

Ordnance Survey Map: OL 7 The English Lakes South-eastern area. *Windermere, Kendal & Silverdale*

The Pub: Tweedies Bar, Red Bank Road, Grasmere, LA22 9SW | 015394 35300 | www.tweediesbargrasmere.co.uk | enquiries@dalelodgehotel.co.uk

Walk outline: Nab Scar lies at the southern end of the long ridge that radiates south from Fairfield. This walk approaches it using the delightful old Corpse Road and then climbing from Rydal. A less well-known path is used for the descent, dropping to Alcock Tarn, tucked into the folds of the fell high above Grasmere.

Part of Grasmere's Dale Lodge Hotel complex, Tweedies Bar has a bright, modern, yet cosy feel to it. Drinkers can enjoy a range of beers from seven hand pumps and a scrumpy tap, while diners can eat in either the bar or the restaurant. The log-burning fire is a welcome sight after a cold winter's walk.

Tweedies Bar

▶ Tweedies Bar at a glance

Open: Sun-Thurs, 12 noon-11pm; Fri & Sat, 12 noon-12pm
Brewery/company: Free house
Real ales: Theakston's Old Peculier, Yates', Cumbrian Legendary Ales and Coniston Brewery beers; local and national guest beers
Food: Mon to Sat, 12-3pm, 6-9pm; Sun, 12-4pm, 6.30-9pm. Good mix of traditional and modern dishes. Booking summer weekends
Rooms: Sixteen en-suite rooms in the adjoining Dale Lodge Hotel
Outside: Spacious beer garden with 30 tables
Children & dogs: Children welcome. In evenings, dogs in bar only

The Walk

1. With your back to **St Oswald's Church**, turn left along the road. At a small roundabout, turn right on to the A591 and then immediately left on to a minor road. You soon pass **Dove Cottage**.

Dove Cottage was William Wordsworth's home from 1799 until 1808, although it has only been known as Dove Cottage since the Wordsworth Trust bought it in 1891. He and his family received many guests here, including Sir Walter Scott, Robert Southey and, their most frequent visitor, the poet Coleridge. After the Wordsworths moved out, the cottage became the home of William's young friend, Thomas de Quincey, although he soon upset the family by making alterations to their beloved garden. Best known for his 1821 work Confessions of an English Opium-Eater, *he lived in Dove Cottage for 22 years, much longer than the Wordsworths.*

Just after passing a lane and small pond on the left, bear left at a fork in the road—signposted to 'Alcock Tarn'. Keep following the surfaced lane, part of the **old Corpse Road**. After passing the last of three slate cottages, it becomes a rough track.

2. As it passes to the right of one more cottage, it narrows; ignore the path to the right here. Follow the track in and out of pretty woodland along the southern slopes of **Nab Scar** and across grazing land with views down to **Rydal Water**. There are a few benches along this stretch of the path, so you can rest and enjoy the scenery.

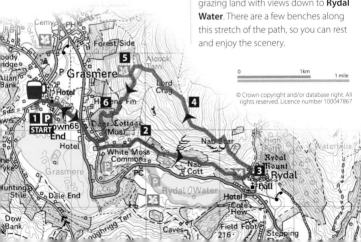

Upland lake: *Mirroring the sky, Alcock Tarn sits on the lower slopes of Heron Pike*

3. Eventually you reach a quiet lane near **Rydal Mount**—another of Wordsworth's homes—along which you turn left. At a fork, follow the concrete track up to the left. Then, as this swings towards a private gate, go through the kissing-gate next to the larger gate up to the right. Keep right at a fork to climb the clear, pitched and often steep path.

This is a busy section of the route, particularly early in the day, when those doing the Fairfield Horseshoe are just setting out on the western arm of the round. So, there'll be plenty of opportunities to stop and chat with fellow walkers as you labour upwards—a good excuse to stop and catch your breath. And, if you're here at a rare quiet time, you can always use the fantastic views down to Rydal Water on the left as your pretext for resting.

After almost one kilometre of ascent, the ridge opens out and the gradient eases.

4. You soon cross a wall via a stone stepped stile. It is important now to count the cairns north of this wall, as

Green vale: *Grasmere village and lake sit side by side in a beautiful green vale*

these hold the key to your descent. The first, about 80 metres beyond the wall, is on a small mound up to the left; the second cairn is actually on the path itself; the third cairn, about 300 metres beyond the wall, is on another mound to the left. About 30 metres after this third cairn, bear left along a faint path heading north-west at first: it has a tiny, guiding cairn close to the start of it. As you descend, you catch occasional glimpses of Alcock Tarn below.

5. The path eventually drops to a wall on the eastern side of **Alcock Tarn**. Cross via a railed gap and bear left to walk along the raised bank on the southern edge of the water.

Straight ahead now are the Langdale Pikes, Bow Fell and Crinkle Crags.

At the far end of this bank, bear left— away from the tarn. The wide, grassy path soon goes through a gap in a wall. Keep to the clearest route as it winds its way downhill, ignoring all trails down to the right. Almost one kilometre after leaving Alcock Tarn, you pass a small, surprisingly deep pool to the left of the path.

6. Soon after this, bear left at a waymarked fork among the trees. The route passes through National Trust woodland at **Brackenfell** and then reaches a surfaced lane. Now retracing your steps from earlier in the walk, turn right and follow the road round to the right. Turn right at the main road and left at the mini roundabout to walk back into **Grasmere**. ♦

Coffin route

The bridleway followed from Grasmere to Rydal at the start of the walk is known as the Corpse Road. Before St Mary's in Ambleside was consecrated, coffins had to be transported to Grasmere for burial. Soon after passing Dove Cottage, you will see a large rock to the left of the road. This is known as the Coffin Stone and was used to support the coffin while the bearers rested.

Langstrath Country Inn, Stonethwaite

Langstrath Country Inn
Borrowdale

What to expect:
Mostly good paths and stony tracks; boggy at times on open fell; steep descent

Distance/time: 8.7km/5.4 miles. Allow 3-3½ hours

Start: Stonethwaite in Borrowdale. The turning for Stonethwaite is about 700 metres on the left after Rosthwaite. Outside of school hours, walkers can use the Borrowdale Church of England Primary School car park. Alternatively, park on the roadside nearby

Grid ref: NY258 139

Ordnance Survey Map: OL4 The English Lakes North-western area. *Keswick, Cockermouth & Wigton*

The Pub: The Langstrath Country Inn, Stonethwaite, Borrowdale, Cumbria CA12 5XG | 01768 777239 | www.thelangstrath.com

Walk outline: Dock Tarn is hidden in a lovely, secluded hollow high above busy Borrowdale. It is reached via a track that climbs gently from the valley floor and then drops to out-of-the-way Watendlath and its eponymous tarn. Moorland paths lead up to Dock Tarn before a steep path drops through oak woods back to Stonethwaite

The Langstrath Country Inn is a family-run pub tucked away in a quiet side valley close to Borrowdale. The cottage was built in 1590, but the building has been converted in a bright, but cosy style. As well as a small bar, there is a dining area with picture windows, providing good views of the fells.

The Langstrath Country Inn

▶ **Langstrath Country Inn at a glance**

Open: April-Nov, Tues-Sun, 12-10.30pm; closed Dec and Jan except New Year; Feb and March, open Fri-Sun only

Brewery/company: Freehouse

Real ales: Old Peculier, Jennings, Keswick Brewery ales

Food: 12-2.30pm and 6-8.30pm with light snacks available at other times. Good menu with an emphasis on local produce.

Rooms: Eight en-suite rooms

Outside: Small beer garden with seven tables

Children & dogs: Children not allowed in dining room after 7.30pm. Dogs allowed only on flagged area of the bar

The Walk

1. From **Borrowdale Primary School**, simply keep following the lane south-east towards **Stonethwaite**, an attractive collection of cottages, farm buildings and a pub. As you enter the hamlet, take the footpath on the left — signposted 'Greenup Edge, Grasmere'. There is an old phone box here.

The footpath is enclosed between walls built from the rounded stones you will see in the riverbed. These would have covered most of the fields at one time.

2. Follow the path over the footbridge and turn left at the T-junction — signposted Watendlath. This path is part of the Cumbria Way so don't be surprised if you encounter exhausted backpackers between here and **Rosthwaite**. The path follows the valley floor parallel to **Stonethwaite Beck** over the wall to the left. As you approach Rosthwaite ignore a promising looking path on the right, keeping to the path ahead.

3. At the bridge in **Rosthwaite** — an alternative starting point for those unable to park near Stonethwaite — and with **Hazel Bank Country House** on the right, take the

bridleway ahead signed to 'Watendlath 1½ miles'. The path passes beside the gardens of Hazel Bank and crosses the stream to begin the climb.

Higher up, at a T-junction immediately after a gate, turn left and continue the steady climb on the good path with widening views behind across **Borrowdale** to **Glaramara**, the **Scafell group**, **Great Gable** and **Dale Head**.

4. When you reach the gate at the top of the hillside most of the ascent is behind you. This leads onto the open fell — a very different landscape

Peaceful scene: *The old stone bridge leading into the hamlet of Watendlath*

to the lower valley with views ahead to **High Seat** and **High Tove**. Continue ahead on the good path soon making a gentle descent to **Watendlath** — a handful of farm buildings nestled beside the tarn. Cross the little stone bridge to reach the tearoom.

5. Cross the bridge again and keep left at the fork — signposted Dock Tarn. The path runs beside the tarn, and then continues as a farm lane between

stone walls. After a gate the path swings up rightwards along the top edge of the field. Ford a **stream** and turn right on a path which climbs steadily to a kissing-gate. After the gate the path bears left, climbing gently again to reach a T-junction on the flatter, open moors. Turn left here, the path crossing patches of boggy ground by stepping stones.

Wide views again open out across Borrowdale to Great Gable, Brandreth and Pillar over the shoulder of Fleetwith Pike beyond the Honister Mines. To the west is the long Dale Head-Maiden Moor ridge.

Sheltered water: *A fly-fisherman at work on the peaceful waters of Watendlath Tarn*

After the next kissing-gate, the pitched path climbs more steeply over rocky ground. The path here is obvious, but very rocky and uneven. Just before you reach **Dock Tarn** you get a view ahead to the broad summits of **Ullscarf** and **High Raise**.

Small, reedy Dock Tarn sits in a hollow surrounded by rocky knolls thickly cloaked in heather, a landscape that looks more like the Scottish hills than the Cumbrian fells. Water lilies grace the surface of the water, starting to flower in the late spring,

and, all around, wispy patches of bog cotton occupy the damp, peaty ground. Later in the summer, the open fells here become a mass of purple as the heather bursts into brief, but beautiful bloom.

6. Follow the obvious footpath beside the tarn. At the far end, this swings right to begin the descent into the valley. Cross a stile with a view ahead up **Langstrath**. The path steepens now, passing a small **stone shelter** soon with a view down into **Stonethwaite**. The path down through the woods is very steep, but is pitched for most of the way. Although this makes it easier, care is needed especially if the stones are wet.

At the lower edge of the woods stone steps take you over a wall. Follow the path ahead through the bracken to join the **Cumbria Way** path along the valley floor. Turn right, then left over the **bridge** to return to Stonethwaite to complete the walk. The **Langstrath Country Inn** is up to the left when you re-enter the hamlet. ♦

Watendlath

The pretty, unspoilt hamlet of Watendlath is hidden high in a hanging valley above Borrowdale. This was the last place in the Lake District to get mains electricity – the lights finally being turned on in 1978. It was the setting for Hugh Walpole's 1931 novel Judith Paris, the second of four books in the Herries Chronicle. These tell the story of a local family from the 18th century to the 1930s depression.

Looking across Crummock Water from the western shore

Kirkstile Inn
Loweswater

What to expect:
Woodland and lakeside paths; good tracks; some road walking

Distance/time: 8.5km / 5¼ miles. Allow 2½-3 hours

Start: Parking area next to Lanthwaite Green Farm near the northern end of Crummock Water, about 4.5km north of Buttermere

Grid ref: NY 159 208

Ordnance Survey Map: OL 4 The English Lakes North-western area. *Keswick, Cockermouth & Wigton*

The Pub: Kirkstile Inn, Loweswater, Cumbria CA13 0RU | 01900 85219 | www.kirkstile.com | info@kirkstile.com

Walk outline: This lovely walk links woodlands close to Crummock Water and the tiny village of Loweswater. It takes in everything from gnarled oaks to conifer stands, where there's a real chance of spotting rare red squirrels. Dropping to the lakeshore, the walk gives outstanding views of the fells surrounding this magnificent lake.

Tucked away between Loweswater and Crummock Water, the Kirkstile Inn is a classic Lakeland pub that has been providing food and shelter since Tudor times. Modern visitors can expect a relaxed atmosphere, low beams, open fires, good food and beer. There are two bars and a comfortable dining room.

Kirkstile Inn

▶ Kirkstile Inn at a glance

Open: Mon-Sat 11am-11pm; Sun 12 noon-10.30pm
Brewery/company: Free house with own brewery
Real ales: Loweswater Gold, Melbreak bitter, Coniston Bluebird, Grasmoor Dark, Yates bitter, guest beers
Food: Daily 12-2pm, 6-9pm. Excellent, rustic dishes with a Cumbrian focus. Specials board. Often busy, booking advisable
Rooms: Four rooms en-suite, plus family annexe
Outside: Lovely beer garden with 20 tables and a play area
Children & dogs: Children welcome. Dogs allowed in bar only

The Walk

1. From the parking area, turn left along the road. Just after the farm, cross the stile on your left. After the path swings right and just before it enters a field, go through the kissing-gate on your left and walk alongside the wall on the right.

2. After entering **Lanthwaite Woods**, follow the track and keep straight ahead at any junctions until you reach the gate leading into the car park. Go through this and continue to the road.

3. Turn left and walk along the asphalt for 700 metres, ignoring the first road junction as you pass the Loweswater sign. Then turn left along the lane signposted to the **Kirkstile Inn**.

4. With the pub directly in front of you, turn left and immediately right. Follow

this lane to a gate in front of a stand of conifers. Go through and take the left fork. As you emerge from the trees, turn left to walk with the fence on your left. The path generally stays close to the fence/wall on the left, but it does briefly swing away from it as it descends.

5. Don't go through the gate in the wall corner near **Highpark**; instead, turn right along a faint, grassy path parallel with the wall on the left. As you look down on **Crummock Water**, bear left—staying with the wall—to descend to the lakeshore. At the water's edge, turn left through the gate. Keep to the lakeshore path, around the side of the **pumphouse** and across some bridges.

6. Soon after the final bridge, you reach a junction of paths near some benches. Take the narrow path on the right. This

Dawn's early light: *A mirror-still sunrise at Crummock Water*

joins a track from the left, which ends at a **boathouse**. A narrow path continues along the lakeshore. After leaving the woods, keep straight ahead. The trail becomes indistinct as it approaches the tumbledown end of a wall, but maintain the same line. After the wall, bear left to climb to the higher of two gates ahead. Beyond this, continue gently uphill. Bear left at a fork to reach a gate beside the road.

7. Turn left and walk along the asphalt for around one kilometre to return to the parking area. ♦

'Deep and solemn'

In his Guide to the Lakes, *the Romantic poet William Wordsworth was struck by the beauty of Crummock Water. "... There is scarcely anything finer than the view from a boat in the centre of Crummock Water," he wrote. "The scene is deep, and solemn and lonely; and in no other spot is the majesty of the mountains so irresistibly felt as an omnipresence, or so passively submitted to as a spirit incumbent upon the imagination."*

Barrow's shapely north-east ridge

Middle Ruddings Inn
Braithwaite

What to expect:
Mostly good paths, but less distinct on Outerside and Stile End

Distance/time: 7.5km / 4¾ miles. Allow 3-3½ hours

Start: Opposite the village of Braithwaite on the A66 there is a loop of the old road with space for several cars

Grid ref: NY238 237

Ordnance Survey Map: OL 4 The English Lakes North-western area. *Keswick, Cockermouth & Wigton*

The Pub: Middle Ruddings Inn, Braithwaite, near Keswick, Cumbria CA12 5RY | 017687 78436 | www.middle-ruddings.co.uk

Walk outline: Barrow's shapely north-east ridge is just crying out to be walked. With excellent views and steep ground tumbling away on either side, giving the fell a sense of airiness that is totally out of proportion to its modest 455m, it is one of the best low-level ridges in the Lake District. Combining it with Outerside and Stile End makes for a great half-day's outing.

More inn than pub, Middle Ruddings is run by Andy and Liz McMaster, a friendly couple who are clearly passionate about their beers and their food. Expect only the best as you unwind in the laid-back lounge or the conservatory restaurant.

On Barrow's summit

▶ **Middle Ruddings Inn at a glance**

Open: Daily 10.30am to 11pm
Brewery/company: Free house
Real ales: Uses only Cumbrian breweries
Food: Daily, 6-9pm; also Sat and Sun, 12-2pm. Booking recommended
Rooms: Fourteen en-suite rooms
Outside: Small terrace and garden at front. Larger garden at rear
Children & dogs: Both welcome to dine or stay

The Walk

1. Cross the busy main road and turn right along the pavement towards Braithwaite. Bear left into the village and walk ahead past '**Scotgate**' caravan and camp site. Bear left along Croft Terrace and at the end turn left over the bridge, signed 'Newlands'.

After the last house on the right (about 150 metres after a small shop), turn right up the driveway to '**Braithwaite Lodge**'. Follow the driveway up to the house and pass to the right of it to cross a stile behind outbuildings. Follow the path up a small field to go through a gate in the wall. Bear left now up on to the ridge.

2. Turn right on a grass path that follows the crest of the ridge with widening views as you climb. The ridge takes you directly to the summit of **Barrow**—just over 1.5 kilometres distant with a climb of 300 metres. There are grand views all the way, especially back to Skiddaw and across the Newlands Valley to Cat Bells.

3. From Barrow's summit, the ridge path drops down to **Barrow Door**, the gap between Barrow and the little summit of Stile End. Bear left here to meet up with the clear path coming up Stonycroft Gill from the left. You now head west, gently uphill, around the southern, rocky flank of **Stile End** and up to a wide flat area named on Ordnance Survey maps as **High Moss**.

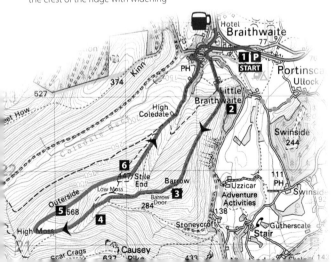

Rolling fells: *Stile End and Causey Pike*

(If you are taking this walk in your stride you can add a few more summits to your list by continuing on the path ahead to reach the ridge between Sail and Scar Crags. From there it is a straightforward walk east along the ridge over Scar Crags and on to Causey Pike. From Causey Pike head back towards Scar Crags and take the path which leaves the ridge on the right about midway between the two summits. This path descends back to High Moss.)

4. As the gradient eases, watch for a ruined sheepfold just to the left of the track. This is the key to the next section of the walk—turn right along a faint path here. You climb a little as the path swings around the south-western end of **Outerside** to reach a slightly clearer path. Turn right here to climb quickly and easily on to the summit of Outerside.

The messy workings on the other side of Coledale belong to the disused Force Crag Mine where lead, zinc and barytes were once mined. A lead vein was located

Coledale: *A view down Coledale to Braithwaite with Skiddaw in the distance*

at Coledale Head in 1578, although concentrated work didn't start until the 19th century. The last attempt to extract ore was made by the New Coledale Mining Company in 1984, but the firm left in 1990.

5. Continue over the summit and steeply down to the broad pass known as **Low Moss** separating Outerside from the final summit of Stile End. The heather-filled depression is boggy in places, but you shouldn't experience any difficulties if you keep to the highest ground. Soon after spying a small, reed-fringed pool to your left, you pass (and ignore) a path heading off to the left at a right angle. The route now climbs slightly before swinging left to skirt a boggy area. It then swings back round to the right to begin the short climb on to **Stile End**. You quickly reach a faint fork where you bear left to keep to the ridge.

6. From the top of Stile End, head north-east down the broad ridge—almost a twin of Barrow's ridge. Partway down, join the path coming in from **Barrow Door** on your right. The path becomes solid underfoot as you pass a track to the ruins of **High Coledale** to your left.

Leave the open fell via a kissing-gate and walk down the lane until you see the Coledale Inn on your left. Turn right here, down the rough track and at the end turn right turn right past the Methodist chapel. Swing left over the bridge and turn right into the village. For the **Middle Ruddings Inn** turn left immediately after the Royal Oak on the Thornthwaite road. ♦

Pencils

The famous Cumberland Pencil Company, established in 1868, was originally located in Braithwaite. It used Borrowdale graphite, first discovered in the early 1500s and known locally as 'wad', to make its world-famous pencils. The company moved to Keswick in 1898 after the Braithwaite factory was destroyed by fire. Although the museum remains in Keswick, the factory has since moved to west Cumbria.

Derwentwater and the Derwent Fells from Walla Crag

Dog & Gun
Keswick

What to expect:
Lakeshore and wood-land trails; good path on fell; town pavements

Distance/time: 10.5km / 6½ miles. Allow 3-4 hours

Start: National Trust car park at Great Wood close to Derwentwater. Around 2km south of Keswick on the B5289, Borrowdale Road

Grid ref: NY 272 214

Ordnance Survey Map: OL 4 The English Lakes North-western area. *Keswick, Cockermouth & Wigton*

The Pub: Dog & Gun, 2 Lake Road, Keswick, Cumbria CA12 5BT
01768 773463 | dogandgun@orchidpubs.co.uk

Walk outline: High above sparkling Derwentwater and with Skiddaw looming nearby, Walla Crag provides some of the best views in the Keswick area. But this route offers so much more: easy walking along the lakeshore, woodland trails and a visit to what must be the most photogenic bridge in the whole of the Lake District.

A town centre venue, the Dog and Gun is a traditional pub with a friendly, homely feel to it. Walkers are always welcome, as are their dogs, who are provided with a special doggy menu of treats and chews. The homemade Hungarian goulash goes down well after a day on the fells.

Dog & Gun, Keswick

▶ Dog and Gun at a glance

Open: Daily, 12 noon-11pm
Brewery/company: Orchid Pubs chain, but not tied to a brewery
Real ales: Theakston's Old Peculier; Yates, Keswick Brewing Company; Cumbrian Legendary Ales; guest ales
Food: Daily, 12-9pm. Hearty, home-made meals; no fried food. No booking
Rooms: None
Outside: No beer garden
Children & dogs: Children only when dining. Dogs welcome

The Walk

1. Walk back to the road from the car park, cross over and follow one of the paths to the shore at **Calfclose Bay**.

The bay is a lovely spot, one of many on the shores of Derwentwater. On a calm, clear day the view across to the shapely Derwent Fells is one of the finest in the Lake District.

Head left along the shore, following the path around a wooded headland. As you approach the road, the path rises up over rocks and there is a lay-by directly opposite. Cross the road and go through a gap in the wall. Take the path which bears half-right past the rocks and up bracken-covered slopes to join a path at a T-junction.

2. Turn right to walk beneath **Falcon Crag**. Keep left at a fork— signposted to 'Ashness Bridge'. Continue ahead, eventually passing through a gate as you approach the road near pretty **Ashness Bridge**.

3. Having visited the bridge, retrace your steps towards the gate, but then take the upper right-hand path—up bracken- covered slopes and through an area of loose rocks. Cross the stile and continue to a T-junction of

paths. Turn left here and follow the path above **Falcon Crag** and high above Derwentwater with spectacular views.

4. The path eventually rounds the head of steep-sided **Cat Gill** on the left, then swings left to a stile over a wall. Cross this and follow the path up onto a viewpoint above **Walla Crag**.

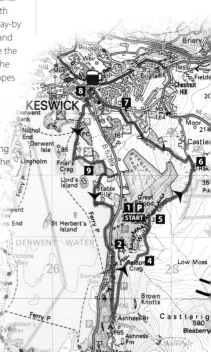

Wooded Isle: *Derwent Isle and Catbells*

This is the high point of the walk, both in altitude and panorama. The view takes in much of Derwentwater, with its scattering of islands, Keswick to the north with Skiddaw rising in a series of rounded buttresses and gullies. On the other side of Derwentwater, you should be able to pick out the familiar profile of Catbells with Causey Pike, Eel Crag and Grizedale Pike.

5. Head away from the top in a north-east direction to follow a path that skirts the edge of the crag and drops to another stile in the wall. After this, turn left and begin your descent, parallel with the drystone wall on your left. This path drops to cross a stream via a footbridge and reaches a lane near **Rakefoot Farm**.

6. Walk down the lane for about 250 metres. Turn sharp left onto a signed path to 'Keswick Great Wood'. Cross the beck again by a footbridge, then turn right and follow the path along the top edge of **Springs Wood** with the beck down to the right. Ignore a path on the left that leads back into **Great Wood**—although this could be used as a shortcut back to the car park if needed.

Perfect reflections: *A flat calm Derwentwater catches perfect reflections of fells, isles and woods, from Calf Close Bay*

Stay with the path where it swings right then left; don't cross the footbridge on the right here. Emerge from the woods to pass **Springs Farm** on the left. Cross the bridge and follow the road ahead towards Keswick.

7. At the end of the road turn left and follow this road all the way into **Keswick**. As you enter the town square, with the **Moot Hall** ahead, bear left and left again to reach **the Dog and Gun**.

8. Turn right as you leave the pub and follow the street to the George Fisher outdoor shop. Turn right here and follow the road at first, then the subway. Bear left at the ice-cream kiosk, eventually passing the **Theatre by the Lake** to reach the landing stages.

Walking the lakeshore track, keep right at a fork. At the end of **Friar's Crag**, turn round and begin heading back the way you came, but then, almost immediately, take a narrow trail on the right heading up to **Ruskin's Monument**, partly concealed by the trees. Now following the path on the eastern side of the crag, walk down the steps and turn right through a gate.

9. The shore path later enters the marshy woodland of **The Ings**. On leaving the woods, turn right along a rough lane. Pass a cottage on the right to reach the shore again and continue to the next wooded headland—**Broom Hill Point**. You are soon back in **Calfclose Bay** where the walk began. Follow one of the paths back to the car park to complete the walk. ♦

Chocolate box bridge

Stone-built Ashness Bridge is certainly one of the most photographed places in the Lake District. Although it is often dismissed as a 'chocolate box' spot today, it easy to see why it once was, and continues to be, so popular. The classic view is from a few metres upstream where the bridge is outlined against a spectacular backdrop of Derwentwater and the impressive bulk of Skiddaw.

Useful Information

Cumbria Tourism
Cumbria Tourism's official website covers everything from accommodation and events to attractions and adventure. **www.golakes.co.uk**

Lake District National Park
The Lake District National Park website also has information on things to see and do, plus maps, webcams and news. **www.lakedistrict.gov.uk**

Tourist Information Centres
The main TICs provide free information on everything from accommodation and travel to what's on and walking advice.

Ambleside	01539 432 582	tic@thehubofambleside.com
Bowness	01539 442 895	bownesstic@lakedistrict.gov.uk
Coniston	01539 441 533	mail@conistontic.org
Keswick	01768 772 645	keswicktic@lakedistrict.gov.uk
Penrith	01768 867 466	pen.tic@eden.gov.uk
Ullswater	01768 482 414	ullswatertic@lakedistrict.gov.uk
Windermere	01539 446 499	info@windermereinfo.co.uk

Cumbrian breweries and pubs
As well as the mainstream Cumbrian breweries such as Jennings, the Lake District supports more than twenty micro-breweries producing award-winning real ales and craft beers, plus five real cider and perry makers.

For details of the encouragingly high number of real ale pubs in the Lake District, see the local CAMRA websites, or buy a copy of their excellent, annual *Good Beer Guide*.

Visitors can also sample a mouth-watering range of local real ales at the many Lakeland beer festivals held throughout the year.

See: **www.camra.org.uk** or **www.cumbriacamra.org.uk**

Weather
Five-day forecast for the Lake District
0844 846 2444 | **www.lakedistrict.gov.uk/visiting/weather-enjoying**